Landings
INTERNATIONAL

A PAULIST MINISTRY OF RECONCILIATION

Participant's Journal

edited by
Thomas A. Kane, CSP

Paulist Press
New York / Mahwah, NJ

NIHIL OBSTAT
Reverend Monsignor C. Anthony Ziccardi, SSL, STD
Censor Librorum for the Archdiocese of Newark
August 16, 2012

IMPRIMATUR
+ Most Reverend John J. Myers, JCD, DD
Archbishop of Newark
August 16, 2012

For more information contact:

LANDINGS International
North American Paulist Center
3015 Fourth Street NE
Washington, DC 20017
202-269-2550

landingsdc@yahoo.com
www.landingsintl.org

Revised 2012

ISBN: 978-0-8091-9684-5

To order materials:

PAULIST PRESS
997 Macarthur Blvd.
Mahwah, NJ 07430
800-218-1903
201-825-7300

info@paulistpress.com
www.paulistpress.com

Published by Paulist Press
Printed and bound in the United States of America

Contents

he Preamble   5

cknowledgments   6

Meeting Schedule   7

heck-In Time   8

eading Prayer   10

elling My Story   12

My Spiritual Story   14

torytelling: Our Response   17

eflection on Catholic Themes   18
- I. Who Is God?   21
- II. Why Follow Jesus?   25
- III. The Holy Spirit and the Church— *1/22/13*   31
- IV. Baptism and Confirmation — *1/29/13*   37
- V. Eucharist and Liturgy   43
- VI. Sin and Reconciliation   49
- VII. Vocation — *2/5*   55
- VIII. Suffering, Death, and Resurrection   61
- IX. The Catholic Life   67
- X. Christian Prayer   75

Closing Prayer   80

The Preamble

Welcome to the beginning of your LANDINGS journey. Hopefully, you will find here the help, peace, and enjoyment thousands of others have found in LANDINGS.

LANDINGS is a uniquely contemporary approach to reconciliation ministry. LANDINGS gives someone who is considering returning to the Church an insight into the actual faith lives of a few other Catholics. LANDINGS is not a discussion group. LANDINGS is not a class. It is an experience of faith sharing.

More than anything else LANDINGS is a ministry of compassionate listening. Some call listening the language of God. Over the course of the weeks ahead, each person, the welcoming Catholic and the returnee, will have ample and equal opportunity to both speak and be heard. Few of us are listened to enough, so we may not know how to limit ourselves when we encounter a receptive audience. The timekeeper plays an important role in helping the group maintain the necessary limits so that everyone can be heard.

Welcoming members are part of the faith-sharing process and are not here to cure, teach, "fix," or in any way sit in judgment of anyone else's opinions or faith stance. Compassionate listening works best when there is no interrupting, arguing, questioning one another, or commenting on what another said.

If you respect the guidelines, enough of your Catholic identity will emerge to provide returning members with a genuine, balanced look into the mind and heart of the Catholic faith as it is lived and expressed in your parish. Those who feel comfortable returning to Communion with the Church discover during the process that they are just as beloved by God, just as Catholic, just as called to holiness as the rest of us.

Confidentiality is essential in LANDINGS. This applies especially to our spiritual autobiographies. Only in an atmosphere of trust will people speak openly and honestly of their lived beliefs.

Remember, LANDINGS has a highly successful track record. We urge you to follow the program as it is written. Its unique structure has been tested and proven effective by hundreds of groups over the past decade. Resist reverting to familiar ways of running a group, or making changes and adaptations as you go along.

Each person's journey is special and sacred in the eyes of God. If you will trust the Holy Spirit and the process, we are confident you will grow in faith and understanding with the passing weeks and be for each other a clear sign of God's ongoing acceptance and unconditional love.

Happy LANDINGS!

†
For Jac and Jim

We especially remember the legacy of the late Father Jac Campbell, CSP,
the founder of LANDINGS, whose heart for those away from the
Church inspired him to start LANDINGS many years ago, and
the late Father James Moran, CSP, who continued his work.
May our ministry continue to reflect their compassionate vision.

Acknowledgments

Thank you to all who contributed to this revised journal:
Anna LaNave, Bill McGarvey, Camille Bissmeyer (principal authors);
with Karen Vittone, Patricia Watson, Steve Petroff, Susan Timoney, and
Georgina Vaca (editorial); and Stefani Manowski (design)

Meeting Schedule

Every LANDINGS meeting focuses on sharing our faith stories and reflecting on Catholic themes. Below is the format and timing we will use for every meeting, as well as the theme for that week.

Please come on time as we will start on time!

There are eight weeks in the "formal" LANDINGS program. This book, your *Participant's Journal,* includes material for two extra weeks if your group would like to continue for one or two more meetings. Even if your group decides not to, please read the material on your own. It's interesting and informative, and it will be a great help on your journey back home.

Meeting schedule—

Check-in time: 20 minutes — *7:10 - 7:30*

Opening prayer leader: 5 minutes *7:30*

Spiritual journey storytelling: 20–30 minutes *7:30 - 8:00*

Response to story: 10 minutes *8:10*

Hospitality break: 10 minutes *8:40*

Reflection on Catholic themes: 20–25 minutes

    ✓ I. Who is God?

    ✓ II. Why Follow Jesus? *Lee*

    ✓ III. The Holy Spirit and the Church — *Joy*

    IV. Baptism and Confirmation

    V. Eucharist and Liturgy

    VI. Sin and Reconciliation

    VII. Vocation — *Jane*

    VIII. Suffering, Death, and Resurrection

    IX. The Catholic Life (optional)

    X. Christian Prayer (optional)

Program facilitator's or leader's reflection: 10 minutes

Housekeeping: 5 minutes

Closing prayer

Check-In Time

This is a brief time for group members to tune into each other's lives and try to bridge the week between meetings. This activity establishes respect for one another's particular state at the time of the group's gathering. It also encourages ease and openness—that is, members don't have to guess the motivation of other group members; for example, if I'm quiet tonight, it's because I have a headache and I'm only operating at 70 percentage, not because I'm unhappy with the group.

It is very important that members are given undivided attention when they are speaking. However, no attempt to solve or fix people's problems are made here in the meeting. Individual follow-up can always occur naturally at the break or after the meeting.

Here are some sample starters for check-in time:

- When were you conscious of God's presence this week?

- Was there a time you felt as though God was speaking to you or acting in your life?

- Was there something at Mass that touched you in a particular way?

- Did you have a meaningful encounter with someone this week or feel touched through an experience with nature?

- Are you excited about having made any strides this week, such as being particularly patient or loving in a difficult instance?

Leading Prayer

Leading prayer might seem a little intimidating, but it doesn't need to be. It's a special time when you are given the opportunity to help your group members to take a moment and open their hearts to God. Each prayer will be unique because of the unique person leading it. There is plenty of room to be creative when facilitating this encounter with God, yet simple prayer is often the most effective. The following is a suggested sequence for prayer.

CENTERING TIME: This allows each person to take the time to silently call to mind God's presence. Creating a serene environment can be very helpful as members try to step away from the hectic details of their day-to-day life and focus on the reality of God's presence. Dimming the lights, lighting a candle, or encouraging the group to breathe deeply in order to relax can assist in setting a prayerful mood.

REFLECTION TIME: This is a short period of input when the member who is leading offers the group food for reflection. What is entailed in this section is limited only by the imagination. For instance, musical selections can be a powerful means of both expression and reflection. Meaningful visuals of all types can also be stimulating. There are also various things that can be read to the group or as a group. The Word of God, or Holy Scripture, is the living revelation of God; thus, the prayer leader is welcome to choose a Scripture passage for meditation. A poem or other reading with a relevant theme is also an option. Simplicity is recommended as it helps to focus the attention as well as facilitate openness to the Spirit's inspiration during the period of prayer. The Church has been immensely blessed by God with many saints, men and women who have gone before us and left us with extraordinary

examples of how to follow Christ. Many saints wrote prayers and spiritual re-flections, and so reading from them, or even from a brief account of a saint's life, can provide inspiration to the group.

RESPONSE TIME: Members may voluntarily use a few minutes to respond to the reflection. Another response option is to provide the group with a prayer that can be read in unison. This type of response could be a short, self-contained prayer, or it could be a litany where the leader reads short prayers of petition or thanksgiving and the group responds together with reciting one phrase at the end of each petition; for example, "We thank you, Lord," or "Open our hearts, Lord."

CONCLUSION: The leader should choose to close the prayer with something simple to signal the transition from awareness of God's presence into a state of readiness for hearing a faith story. This can be as simple as praying the Hail Mary, or saying, "In Jesus' name we pray, Amen." Below is a list of online resources if you need ideas for leading a prayer session or are just looking for new ways to draw closer to God in prayer:

www.catholic.org/prayers

www.ewtn.com/devotionals/prayers/index.htm

www.scborromeo.org/prayers.htm

www.usccb.org/nab/today.shtml—daily Mass readings

www.saintoftheday.org or www.saintoftheday.com—brief description of a saint's life with audio

www.comepraytherosary.org

Telling My Story

If God made human beings because God loved stories, then creation is a success. For humankind is addicted to stories. No matter our mood, in reverie or expectation, panic or peace, we can be found stringing together incidents, and unfolding episodes. We turn our pain into narratives so we can bear it; we turn our ecstasy into narrative so we can prolong it...we tell our stories to live" (John Shea, *Stories of God*).

This is an invitation to you to tell your story. We, the Christian community, need to hear *your* part of our common faith story. Will you share with us how God has been active in your life?

The following questions are meant to help your reflection. You may have other issues that have shaped your life. Go with the questions/themes that are most meaningful to you.

1. Begin with a word or two about the faith lives of your grandparents and your parents. Then consider what important events, people, and situations have shaped your own life. You may want to start at the

beginning or halfway through, or you may want to begin in the present and flash backward. Do whatever best helps you tell your story.

2. What was your early Church experience?

3. What provoked you to leave the Church? What were some of the good times and bad times, highs and lows, in your journey?

4. Can you name the hunger, sense of loss, or something hoped for that drew you to, or back to, the Church?

5. Who and what helped you on the return journey? Who and what did not help?

6. From where do you draw strength?

CAUTION: Share only as much of your story as you feel comfortable telling your group. As a listener in this group, respect confidentiality by being very careful with the gift of another's story.

7. Turn the page for space to write your story.

My Spiritual Story

My Spiritual Story cont'd. Use as much or as little space as you need.

My Spiritual Story cont'd.

Storytelling: Our Response

When someone has shared a personal faith journey with us, we are in a privileged position. In a sense, it is like being invited into someone's home, but instead we are invited into someone's life. When this happens, we instinctively know we are standing on holy ground. Sometimes that awareness can make us tongue-tied. How do we respond? Or do we respond at all? As in the home invitation, we could respond with simple gratitude, or we could comment on what struck us or what we most identified with from our own life experience.

The following reflection questions are suggestions for how to listen and respond to people's stories:

1. What point in this person's story do I identify with the most?

2. Why does this part of his or her story move me?

3. Is there a connection between this person's story and my story?

4. What is God saying to me through this person's story?

5. How can I let the person telling the story know that I appreciate or identify with the gift of his or her story?

Remember, these questions are just suggestions. Placing yourself inside the life of the storyteller will yield your own insights and faith-awareness—trust those insights!

When the storyteller is done, everyone should try to say something in response.

Examples:

Thank you for sharing your story. I appreciate….
Thank you. I could identify with….
Thank you. I admire how you….
Thank you. You reminded me of….
Thank you.

Reflection on Catholic Themes

In the "Telling My Story" section, we reflected individually on our faith journeys and tried to become more aware of God's presence in our lives. We were reminded that the Catholic faith is not just a set of doctrines, but a relationship between each of us and a loving God. For Catholic Christians, the Church is not just a building or an institution. The Church is a living, relational reality. It is the People of God and the Body of Christ.

or many in the LANDINGS program, the opportunity to simply and honestly tell their own story within a Catholic parish setting is a revelation in and of itself. They often express surprise that their experiences are met with compassion and understanding rather than judgment. Some returnees have also asked for information on basic Catholic teachings as they consider a return to the Church. This "Reflection on Catholic Themes" section will enable you to reflect on some of the basic beliefs of Catholicism—via the *Catechism* and Scripture—through the lens of your own personal experiences.

Hopefully, the topics you will encounter over the next few weeks will help you engage and understand Catholic beliefs in your own life as an adult. We will consider how these beliefs impact our lives—our own personal stories.

How to Prepare

Consider each upcoming topic during the week before the meeting. The background material is intended to give you an introduction to the topic as preparation for sharing your thoughts. Then, take some time to focus on the reflection questions (in italics). The evening's discussion will start with the facilitator asking the group one of these questions. Jot down in the book some of your own thoughts about how you would answer these reflection questions. Remember: there are no right answers to these reflection questions, just your own lived experience of the faith. Be honest about your own questions and struggles. You may be surprised how many in your group may share the same concerns.

Further Study

Some participants become particularly interested in investigating a topic even after the discussion. In order to facilitate their exploration, we've provided the ADDITIONAL RESOURCES section at the end of each weekly segment. This section contains additional resources from three different areas of inquiry—the *Catechism*, Scripture, and Church documents (most of the citations we include will be available online):

FROM THE *CATECHISM*: The *Catechism of the Catholic Church* is available online at http://www.usccb.org/catechism/index.shtml. (CCC is the abbreviation for the *Catechism* and is followed by the relevant paragraph or article number.)

FROM SCRIPTURE: The translation of the Bible used for the readings at Mass and approved for Catholics is the *New American Bible*, Revised Edition. It is also available at http://www.usccb.org/nab/bible/index.shtml.

FROM CHURCH DOCUMENTS: This section includes papal encyclicals, pronouncements, Council documents, and other writings. The name of each is followed by the relevant paragraph or article number. Most will be available at the Vatican Web site: http://www.vatican.va/. (This Web site is comprehensive but difficult to search. To find the document, conduct a search for the title in your own search engine, and the Vatican link will usually be the first one listed.)

I. Who Is God?

Despite what some of us may have been taught or experienced in our own lives, Christians believe that a loving God created the world freely out of nothing, for the purpose of allowing his creatures to share in his being, wisdom, and goodness (CCC 295). Sadly, it is all too often a revelation to some that Christians believe that God isn't simply a detached deity who set the world in motion and is no longer concerned but instead is deeply involved in our world and our own lives. Christians believe that God continues to sustain and uphold creation. We believe human beings are created in God's image, body and soul, to share eternally in this life of love.

This sense of God's intimate connection with us and our lives is evident throughout Scripture in passages that reveal that God knew us each personally from the beginning—"Before I formed you in the womb I knew you" (Jeremiah 1:5)—and that he has a plan for each one of us—"For surely I know the plans I have for you, says the LORD, plans for your welfare and not harm, to give you a future with hope" (Jeremiah 29:11).

This opportunity for relationship with God is always before us, and yet—just as in many of our human relationships—we are often tempted to try to find happiness elsewhere. We sometimes look to live in a world without God. We might seek satisfaction in material things, accomplishments, and relationships, but we often notice a restlessness in our hearts and minds. St. Augustine writes, "You have made us for yourself, O God. Our hearts are restless until they rest in you." God is constantly reaching out to us to satisfy this spiritual hunger and thirst we feel. Just as a lover tries to evoke a response in the beloved, so does God seek to awaken the gift of faith within us.

It might be helpful to you to think of this as an invitation. God created each of us with free will. Though human beings can forget or reject God's invitation to them, he desires that each of us find fulfillment and happiness. That is why Christians believe God perpetually calls every one of us in our daily lives by the work of the Holy Spirit. That might sound overly mystical, but all it essentially means is that God's grace is present to us in the everyday aspects of our lives; it is our job to get better at sharpening our ability to recognize God's work in the world we inhabit 24/7. Each of us needs to respond to this invitation and seek God, not half-heartedly, but with our whole hearts, minds, and wills (CCC 30).

When we say that God is a holy mystery, we don't mean that God is a mystery we can never come to know, but a divine truth that invites us to communion, friendship, and unconditional love.

Reflection Questions

Has your image of God changed over the years? If so, how?

How have you experienced God in your life?

"God is love, and he who abides in love abides in God, and God abides in him" (1 John 4:16). Is your life shaped by a Christian belief that "God is love"? If not, why?

Who had the greatest influence on your perception of God? Family? Friends? Clergy?

Are there any obstacles in your life that prevent you from having an intimate relationship with God?

How would you imagine an "intimate relationship with God"? What do you think it would look like FOR YOU?

My Reflections

My Reflections cont'd.

II. Why Follow Jesus?

It's a fair question. After all, we live in an age in which there are endless options and countless competing claims of "truth." How can we possibly determine what is authentic and what isn't? What makes Jesus of Nazareth unique? Sadly, it isn't hard to find people who invoke Jesus' name for purposes that seem to be at odds with the message of the Gospel. Sadly, it also isn't hard to see how institutional scandal has damaged the Church's credibility. Given all these factors, it isn't surprising that an increasing number of Americans consider themselves spiritual but don't identify with any specific religious tradition.

But while these are all real concerns that a mature believer needs to consider, they are by no means the whole story. The Christian faith journey involves critical thought and reasoning, but ultimately it is not simply an intellectual exercise. Last week, your group discussed how we were created to be in relationship with God. Relationships require more than just our minds. At their deepest they engage us beyond simple rationality and connect us intimately with our capacity for love and hope. In the same way, the fundamental grounding of Christianity involves a real relationship with Jesus.

"Being Christian is not the result of an ethical choice or a lofty idea, but the encounter with an event, a person [Jesus Christ] which gives life a new horizon and decisive direction" (Benedict XVI, *God Is Love*).

"As Jesus passed on from there, he saw a man named Matthew [who was a tax collector], sitting at his customs post. He said to him, 'Follow me.' And he got up and followed him" (Matthew 9:9).

As Christians we believe that when the divine entered human history in the person of Jesus, it altered the human story forever. His life, death, and Resurrection, his victory over sin and death, are the most important events in history. Through those events, Jesus showed us that God's love and forgiveness extends to all his children. This week you are invited to discuss the person of Jesus Christ and his mission of God's love for us.

Who?

In discussing "Why follow Jesus?" it will be helpful to ask a related question: "Who is this Jesus?" Vast libraries have been written about this topic, but the Gospels themselves give us the best window into who Jesus was, whom he spent time with, and what he cared about.

Jesus fed five thousand people miraculously with five loaves and two fishes. He said, "I am the bread of life....Whoever eats this bread will live forever; and the bread that I will give is my flesh for the life of the world...." Many left scandalized. He said to the twelve, "Do you also want to leave?" Simon Peter answered him, "Master, to whom shall we go? You have the words of eternal life" (John 6:1–15, 35, 51, 66–68).

Out of love for us, Jesus, innocent of any crime, allowed himself to be brutally crucified as an unblemished sacrifice for the sins of the world. What are the costs of following Jesus in our own lives? Are we able to sit at the foot of the cross as Mary and John did, or do we distance ourselves from this Suffering Servant, hiding away, afraid of the costs of following him? Jesus said, "If any want to become my followers, let them deny themselves, take up their cross, and follow me" (Matthew 16:24).

The other disciples told Thomas that Jesus was raised from the dead. Thomas did not believe. Jesus came, although the doors were locked, and stood in their midst and said, "Peace be with you." Then he said to Thomas, "Put your finger here and see my hands, put it into my side, and do not be unbelieving, but believe." Thomas answered and said to him, "My Lord and my God!" Jesus said to him, "Have you come to believe because you have seen me? Blessed are those who have not seen and have believed" (John 20:24–29).

Jesus said, "I am the way, the truth, and the life" (John 14:6). How have you "met Jesus" in your life? Who do you say Jesus is? What is your relationship with him?

Additional Resources

FROM THE *CATECHISM*

Though divine, the Son of God humbled himself and became human; he was conceived by the Holy Spirit and born of the Virgin Mary. This mystery of our faith is called "the Incarnation" (CCC 456). The Father sent his Son into the world to restore humanity's relationship with God which had been severed by sin so that we would know God's unimaginable love. "For God so loved the world, that he gave his only Son, that everyone who believes in him might not perish but have eternal life" (John 3:16). As St. Thomas Aquinas explains: "The Son of God, wanting to make us sharers in his divinity, assumed our nature, so that he, made man, might make men gods" (CCC 460). Jesus' time on earth was important not only because of his suffering, death, and Resurrection, but also because he became our supreme model of love, forgiveness, and holiness. "The whole of Christ's life was a continual teaching: his silences, his miracles, his gestures, his prayer, his love for people, his special affections for the little and the poor" (CCC 561). To be a follower of Christ is to try to offer compassion, mercy, love, and service to others.

Man (Creation)—CCC 355–384

The Fall—CCC 385–421

"I believe in Jesus Christ the only Son of God"—CCC 422–682

Christ's Redemptive Death—CCC 595–630

Christ's Resurrection and Ascension—CCC 638–667

FROM SCRIPTURE

Mark 9:7—"Then a cloud came, casting a shadow over them; then from the cloud came a voice, 'This is my beloved Son. Listen to him.'"

John 13:15—"I have given you a model to follow, so that as I have done for you, you should also do."

Matthew 11:28–30—Jesus said, "Come to me, all you who labor and are burdened, and I will give you rest. Take my yoke upon you and learn from me, for I am meek and humble of heart, and you will find rest for yourselves. For my yoke is easy, and my burden light."

FROM CHURCH DOCUMENTS

John Paul II. *On Redemption and the Dignity of the Human Race (Redemptor Hominis)*, 1979.

Benedict XVI, *Jesus of Nazareth*, 2007.

Reflection Questions

Jesus asked his disciples: "Who do you say that I am?" Peter responded: "You are the Messiah, the Son of the living God" (Matthew 16:16). If Jesus asked you that same question today, in your own words, how would you respond to him?

Which Gospel passage or event is especially meaningful to you, and why?

Do any Gospel passages confuse or trouble you? Which ones? Why?

Growing up, what was your image of Jesus? What do you think contributed to your feelings about him?

Is your image of Jesus different today? If yes, how? And why do you think this image changed?

If there are so many religions to choose from, why follow Jesus? What motivates you to turn to Jesus?

My Reflections

My Reflections cont'd.

III. The Holy Spirit and the Church

I am spiritual, but not religious."

It is a common sentiment. One survey published in 2010 found that almost 75 percent of 18-to-29-year-olds agree that they are more spiritual than religious. They believe in a God or a spiritual force, but don't belong to any religious group. For them, living their faith is a private matter. Institutions and dogma are a distraction from the core of their belief. But Jesus did not see the Church as an afterthought. He saw it as necessary to continuing his mission to spread the Gospel. Before the risen Christ left this world to be with the Father, he promised the disciples that he would send the Holy Spirit to remain with them forever, and he gave them a mission, "the Great Commission," to go out and tell others the Good News of the Gospel.

"Go therefore and make disciples of all nations, baptizing them in the name of the Father, and of the Son, and of the Holy Spirit, and teaching them to obey everything that I have commanded you. And remember, I am with you always, to the end of the age" (Matthew 28:19–20).

Last week you reflected on how a Christian's faith involves an encounter with the person of Jesus. While that encounter is an intimately personal experience, we are not called to live our faith alone; it can't be lived out in isolation. When Jesus established his Church to continue his presence in the world, he promised that the Holy Spirit would remain with the Church and help it to be faithful to him. We share the Church's mission to follow Jesus and spread his love to the ends of the earth. Through our Baptism we become part of a larger story…a larger set of relationships. That is why Christians refer to themselves as members of the Body of Christ. With the help of the Holy Spirit we become Jesus' arms, legs, ears, eyes, and heart here on earth. What is the Spirit's role in our lives and in the Church's mission on earth? How does being part of the Church strengthen us in our Christian mission?

When Was the Church Established?

The Feast of Pentecost is known as the birthday of the Church. On that day, in the Upper Room, the Holy Spirit came down upon the apostles and Mary, and gave them courage to leave their hiding place and boldly witness to God's love through Christ. The Church does not just have a mission; the Church exists to *be* Mission—the real presence of Jesus Christ to a world in need of salvation and healing.

Christians believe that the Holy Spirit—the third person of the Trinity—is the unity of love between the Father and the Son, and is the abiding presence of Jesus among us.

That same Spirit is also given to each of us, conferring upon us the special spiritual gifts of consolation, peace, joy, and courage that are the fruits of the Spirit and are to be used to help build up the Church. The Holy Spirit also helps us to pray and discern God's will in our lives.

It is important to keep in mind that the Catholic Church is much more than a visible institution, with grand cathedrals and a hierarchical structure and leadership. The Church is one, holy, catholic (meaning "universal"), and apostolic. We are an apostolic community because we believe that our faith was handed down to us by the apostles. The pope himself is considered the successor to St. Peter, the rock upon whom Jesus established his Church. As the Body of Christ, Catholics believe the Church is guided by the Holy Spirit to advance the truths contained in the life and teachings of Jesus.

This mystical reality makes it more than a club that we join. As members of the Church through Baptism, we are truly the "People of God" and temples of the Holy Spirit, part of the universal community of believers (CCC 752). Being part of this community of believers not only links us to others in our own time and place, it also connects us to men and women down through history known as the "communion of saints." This is the bond of "communion between holy persons (*sancti*)" united to and in Christ. These people include 1) those of us who are pilgrims on earth journeying toward our heavenly home; 2) those who are in purgatory undergoing purification before seeing God face to face; and 3) those in heaven enjoying the glory of God's presence and interceding for us. We all form one family, one Church in Christ to praise and glorify God (*Compendium of the Catechism of the Catholic Church* [from now on "Comp."] 194–195; CCC 946–962).

Additional Resources

FROM THE *CATECHISM*

We profess in the Creed that the Church is one, holy, catholic, and apostolic. While enjoying a great diversity in gifts and offices within its people, it is one and holy because its founder and source is Christ. It is catholic (or "universal") because it contains the "fullness of the means of salvation" and is on a mission directed toward the entire human race. The Church is apostolic because it is founded on the faith passed down by the apostles and continues to be guided by their successors: the bishops, assisted by priests, in union with the successor of Peter, the Pope (CCC 811–857).

"I Believe in the Holy Spirit"—CCC 687–747

The Church in God's Plan—CCC 751–780

The Church: People of God, Body of Christ, Temple of the Holy Spirit—CCC 781–810

The Church's Hierarchy—CCC 874–896

The Communion of Saints—CCC 946–962

FROM SCRIPTURE

Romans 12:4–6—"For just as we have many members in one body and all the members do not have the same function, so we, who are many, are one body in Christ, and individually members one of another. Since we have gifts that differ according to the grace given to us, each of us is to exercise them accordingly...."

Matthew 16:17–19—The Holy Spirit strengthens the successor of Peter in a special way to lead the Church: "Jesus said to him in reply, 'Blessed are you, Simon, son of Jonah. For flesh and blood has not revealed this to you, but my heavenly Father. And so I say to you, you are Peter, and upon this rock I will build my Church.'"

FROM CHURCH DOCUMENTS

Because the Holy Spirit founded the Church and continues to dwell within the Church, as well as within the heart of every believer, we can know that Church teaching is reliable. "By this appreciation of the faith, aroused and sustained by the Spirit of truth, the People of God, guided by the sacred teaching authority (magisterial), and obeying it, receives not the mere word of men, but truly the word of God (1 Thessalonians 2:13), the faith once for all delivered to the saints (Jude 3)" (*Lumen Gentium*, 12).

Reflection Questions

*When you hear the term **Church**, what image comes to mind?*

Have you ever experienced Church in a way that went beyond a simple building or structure?

Have you ever associated Church with an individual or family member?

How have you experienced the Holy Spirit in your own life?

Do you recall experiencing the Holy Spirit profoundly during an event or when receiving one of the sacraments? Have you felt consolation, peace, joy, or courage?

My Reflections

My Reflections cont'd.

IV. Baptism and Confirmation

The Christian story is ultimately a salvation story. But what does that often-overused term—to be "saved"—actually mean? To be saved is to live in a loving relationship with God, to seek God's forgiveness when one fails to abide in love, and to persevere in that relationship until death, even when it involves bearing life's crosses (as it inevitably will). It is a process, not a moment in time. As every story—and relationship—has a beginning, every Christian's story begins with the sacrament of Baptism. In Baptism, we became a Christian and part of God's family. This new identity and its calling must be embraced and lived, which is not always easy, so we are also confirmed and strengthened in it through the sacrament of Confirmation.

This relationship can be a source of true joy—a river of consolation and peace of soul, even during times of oppression and anxiety. But, like any living thing, it shouldn't be taken for granted; it must be tended to. A muscle, if not exercised, will eventually weaken and atrophy. The sacraments of Baptism and Confirmation are outward signs of the renewal, strengthening, and transformation that must continually take place on our journey. Salvation is not something we possess, as though it were a gem that we were given and locked up for safekeeping. As Catholic writer Mark Shea explains, salvation is a process: "It begins with faith in Jesus Christ and Baptism, but it does not end there."

An adult convert tells the story of her Easter Vigil reception into the Church:

> *"I baptize you in the name of the Father, the Son, and the Holy Spirit."*
>
> *When the priest spoke those words and poured water over me, I was like the olive branch St. Paul describes (Romans 11:24), grafted onto the People of God, and so becoming incorporated into the Body of Christ. I made a confession of faith and was washed clean, and sealed for and in Christ, through the action of the Holy Spirit working through the priest's words and the water.*
>
> *This momentous event was only the beginning of my being cleansed and nourished by the sacramental life of the Church as I continue my journey to eternal life. As someone who was baptized as an adult I find it beautiful that many parents want to start their children on the road to heaven and bring them into the Church through Baptism, making—along with the community of faith—a confession of faith on their child's behalf. Thanks to their love, the love of the Holy Trinity lives in each baptized Christian.*

Confirmation

As we discussed last week, before he ascended into heaven Jesus promised his disciples that the Holy Spirit would come to them. "You will receive power when the Holy Spirit comes upon you, and you will be my witnesses in Jerusalem, throughout Judea and Samaria, and to the ends of the earth" (Acts 1:8). This occurred forty days later at Pentecost in the Upper Room, when they were filled with the Holy Spirit and received the courage to witness to the Gospel of Jesus Christ.

The Holy Spirit is the living presence of God in our lives, in the Church, and in the world. At the sacrament of Confirmation, we are given another spiritual seal of the Holy Spirit that perfects the sacramental graces received in Baptism. Through Confirmation, we are united more firmly to Christ and strengthened to live more fully as sons and daughters of the Father. We are also given the specific gifts of the Holy Spirit, such as wisdom and courage, in order to bear witness to the Church and to the Christian faith in both words and deeds.

Additional Resources

FROM THE *CATECHISM*

Three sacraments establish the foundations of Christian life: Baptism, the Eucharist, and Confirmation. Sacraments are signs of grace, given to us by Christ and entrusted to the Church, by which divine life is given to us (CCC 1131). They are encounters for us with God, through the Holy Spirit, leading to a deeper, loving union with the Lord and the Body of Christ (the Church). The faithful are born anew in Baptism, strengthened by Confirmation, and in the Eucharist receive the food of eternal life (CCC 1212, 1275).

Baptism also gives each person a share in the priestly, kingly, and prophetic offices of Christ (the priesthood of all believers) whereby we as laypeople help, through our actions and witness, to preach the Gospel. A baptized person receives the gifts of the Holy Spirit and belongs forever to Christ; his or her soul bears a seal or character that cannot be removed (CCC 1262–1274, 1279–1280).

A very common question is whether a person can be saved without Baptism. The *Catechism* explains that "since Christ died for the salvation of all, those can be saved without Baptism who die for the faith (Baptism of blood). Catechumens and all those who, even without knowing Christ and the Church, still (under the impulse of grace) sincerely seek God and strive to do his will can also be saved without Baptism (Baptism of desire)" (CCC 1258–1260).

The Sacrament of Baptism—CCC 1213–1284

The Sacrament of Confirmation—CCC 1285–1321

FROM SCRIPTURE

Romans 6:4–6—"We were indeed buried with him through Baptism into death, so that, just as Christ was raised from the dead by the glory of the Father, we too might live in newness of life. For if we have grown into union with him through a death like his, we shall also be united with him in the Resurrection. We know that our old self was crucified with him, so that our sinful body might be done away with, that we might no longer be in slavery to sin."

Mark 10:39—They said to him, "We are able." And Jesus said to them, "The cup that I drink you shall drink; and you shall be baptized with the Baptism with which I am baptized."

John 3:3–5—Jesus answered and said to him, "Truly, truly, I say to you, unless one is born again he cannot see the kingdom of God." Nicodemus said to him, "How can a man be born when he is old? He cannot enter a second time into his mother's womb and be born, can he?" Jesus answered, "Truly, truly, I say to you, unless one is born of water and the Spirit he cannot enter into the kingdom of God."

Mark 13:11—Jesus said: "When they arrest you and hand you over, do not worry beforehand about what you are to say, but say whatever is given you in that hour; for it is not you who speak, but it is the Holy Spirit."

Galatians 3:26–27—"For in Christ Jesus you are all children of God through faith. As many of you as were baptized into Christ have clothed yourselves with Christ."

FROM CHURCH DOCUMENTS

John Paul II, *Apostolic Exhortation on the Vocation and Mission of the Lay Faithful in the Church and the World (Christifideles Laici)*, 1988.

Reflection Questions

Does being a baptized Catholic make a difference in your daily life? In the life of your family? If so, how? If not, why doesn't it?

Describe one thing that was memorable for you at the last Baptism you attended. Do you know anyone who has been baptized as an adult? What was that experience like?

Have you had a child of your own baptized "in the faith"? What were your thoughts about the process?

Why do you think the Catholic Church baptizes infants?

Aside from the Church or sacraments, in what area of your life, such as family, work, or community, have you felt a true sense of God's grace and blessing?

Have you ever felt strengthened with courage at a moment when it was particularly difficult to live your faith or fulfill your responsibilities? How does Confirmation strengthen you to be a better witness to Christ?

My Reflections

Spiritual Conversion

My Reflections cont'd.

V. Eucharist and Liturgy

Two thousand years after the Passover meal that Jesus celebrated with his twelve disciples on the eve of his crucifixion, there are nearly 1.2 billion people stretching to every corner of the globe who share the Catholic faith.

It is an awesome testament to how seriously our ancestors in faith took Jesus' words in Matthew's Gospel: "Go therefore and make disciples of all nations." With that Passover meal he shared with his friends in Jerusalem two millennia ago, Jesus instituted the sacrament of the Eucharist in which he continually comes and gives himself to us. Through our participation in Mass, we share Christ's sacrificed Body and Blood; we are nourished by it and become what we receive (the Body of Christ). This week we will review the teachings about this essential sacrament that is often referred to as the "source and summit" of the Catholic faith.

By the power of the Holy Spirit, Christ is present to us in several ways during Mass, including the proclamation of God's Word, the Eucharistic assembly (those of us gathered for Mass), and the person of the priest. But above all, Christ is present in the Eucharist itself. That is why the Eucharist is also referred to as "the Real Presence," because Jesus is wholly and entirely present to us in a very special way.

In Church circles, you may have heard the term *transubstantiation* being discussed. Catholics believe that during Mass bread and wine are really changed into the Body and Blood of Christ. This process is called transubstantiation. What does that mean? Our senses tell us that what we see and touch is bread and wine, but our faith tells us that beneath those appearances is a different reality: it is the person of Jesus, Body and Blood, Soul and Divinity (CCC 1381). The Lord invites and urges us to receive him in the sacrament of the Eucharist: "Truly, I say to you, unless you eat the flesh of the Son of Man and drink his blood, you have no life in you" (John 6:53; CCC 1384).

Participating in Mass is central to being Catholic. Like much of our faith life, receiving the Eucharist is not a solitary experience. Those who receive the Eucharist are united more closely to Christ and likewise become his Mystical Body, the Church. We join our prayers with the prayers of the universal Church and we become what we receive.

Liturgy is a gift —
" of the Word — us Communicating to The
" celebration " of the Sacraments
If we open out hearts — God is listening
He will show us the way

Some Reflections on the Sacrament of the Eucharist

"If you are the body and members of Christ, then it is your sacrament that is placed on the table of the Lord; it is your sacrament that you receive. To that which you are, you respond 'Amen' ('yes, it is true!') and by responding to it you assent to it. For you hear the words, 'the Body of Christ' and respond 'Amen.' Be then a member of the Body of Christ that your *Amen* may be true" (St. Augustine, as cited in CCC 1396).

"The Body and Blood of Christ are given to us so that we ourselves will be transformed in our turn. We are to become the Body of Christ, his own Flesh and Blood. We all eat the one bread, and this means that we ourselves become one…God no longer simply stands before us as the One who is totally Other. He is within us, and we are in him. His dynamic enters into us and then seeks to spread outwards to others until it fills the world" (Benedict XVI, World Youth Day, August 21, 2005).

"At the Last Supper, on the night he was betrayed, our Savior instituted the Eucharistic sacrifice of his Body and Blood; he did this in order to perpetuate the sacrifice of the cross through the centuries until he should come again and in this way to entrust to his Beloved Bride the Church a memorial of his death and Resurrection: a sacrament of love, a sign of unity, a bond of charity, a paschal banquet in which Christ is eaten, the heart is filled with grace, and a pledge of future glory is given" (*Constitution on the Sacred Liturgy* 47).

Additional Resources

FROM THE *CATECHISM*

The Holy Eucharist—CCC 1322–1419

FROM SCRIPTURE

John 6:35–58—The "Bread of Life" Discourse

John 6:54–58—"Whoever eats my flesh and drinks my blood has eternal life, and I will raise him on the last day. For my flesh is true food, and my blood is true drink. Whoever eats my flesh and drinks my blood remains in me and I in him. Just as the living Father sent me and I have life because of the Father, so also the one who feeds on me will have life because of me. This is the bread that came down from heaven. Unlike your ancestors who ate and still died, whoever eats this bread will live forever."

John 6:66–69—As a result of this [Jesus' teaching about his being the bread of life], many of his disciples returned to their former way of life and no longer accompanied him. Jesus then said to the twelve, "Do you also want to leave?" Simon Peter answered him, "Master, to whom shall we go? You have the words of eternal life. We have come to believe and are convinced that you are the Holy One of God."

Luke 22:19–20—"Then he took the bread, said the blessing, broke it, and gave it to them, saying, 'This is my body, which will be given for you; do this in memory of me.' And likewise the cup after they had eaten, saying, 'This cup is the new covenant in my blood, which will be shed for you.'" [See also Mark 14:22–24 and Matthew 26:26–28.]

1 Corinthians 10:16—"The cup of blessing that we bless, is it not a participation in the blood of Christ? The bread that we break, is it not a participation in the body of Christ?"

FROM CHURCH DOCUMENTS

John Paul II, *On the Eucharist* (*Ecclesia de Eucharistia*), 2003.

Reflection Questions

What was your understanding of the Eucharist as a child?

What does the Eucharist mean to you now as an adult? How has your understanding of the Eucharist changed over the years and why?

What has been your most recent experience of the Mass? Is it different from when you were a child? In what way is it different? What part of the Mass is most meaningful for you?

When we receive Communion, we are challenged to be like Christ in our thoughts and our actions. How does receiving Christ in the Eucharist and participating in the Mass challenge you personally?

My Reflections

My Reflections cont'd.

VI. Sin and Reconciliation

What is sin? In an age such as ours in which our understanding of human behavior and psychology continually deepens, has sin become an outmoded concept? The stereotype of the fire-and-brimstone preacher exhorting people to "repent or risk eternal damnation!" is well known, but beyond that simplistic rendering, what does it mean to sin in the twenty-first century? If, as we've done throughout these weeks, we think of faith in terms of our relationship with God, then sin can best be thought of as those actions that move us further away from that relationship.

We sin when we reject God's grace in our lives. We may choose our own comfort and pleasure over the needs of others and value the things of this world (wealth, power, honor) over the spiritual, rejecting God's call in our lives. We may ignore God's greatest commandments to love God above all else and our neighbor as ourselves. As we try to follow Christ, we will sometimes fail to act or think in a loving manner. Fortunately, Jesus, through the ministry of the Church, has given us a means of pouring out his mercy for us that enables us to reconcile our relationship. Through the sacrament of Reconciliation (Confession or Penance) we can be granted forgiveness for our failings and the grace to "go and sin no more."

This sense of being in "right relationship" with God is best illustrated in the parable Jesus tells about the Prodigal Son. We can all relate at times to the son who takes his share of his father's wealth, moves away, and squanders it all. The point of the story though is not to caution us against wealth and foolishness; the point is to allow us to witness the deep and abiding love and forgiveness of the son's father.

While the son was still a way off, his father caught sight of him, and was filled with compassion. He ran to his son, embraced him, and kissed him. His son said to him, "Father, I have sinned against heaven and against you; I no longer deserve to be called your son." But his father ordered, "Then let us celebrate with a feast, because this son of mine was dead, and has come to life again; he was lost, and has been found" (Luke 15:20–24).

With this parable, Jesus offers us a glimpse into who God is and how he loves. He is a God who, upon the sight of his lost child, is filled with compassion and then runs to him and kisses him. Jesus' Father is passionate about his children and is always ready to welcome us back with boundless love, compassion, and forgiveness.

In the Gospels, Jesus healed people physically but on a deeper level the people he encountered were healed and made whole in a spiritual sense. "The Lord Jesus Christ, physician of our souls and our bodies…has willed that his Church continue, in the power of the Holy Spirit, his work of healing and salvation" (CCC 1421). *The sacrament of Penance + the sacrament of the anointing of the sick*

But if it is only God who forgives sin, why do we tell our sins to a priest? Why don't we simply tell them to God directly and skip the "middle man"? Jesus entrusted the power of absolution to the apostles and instituted the sacrament of Penance by which the baptized are offered conversion, forgiveness, and healing. "As the Father has sent me, so I send you....Receive the Holy Spirit. Whose sins you forgive are forgiven them, and whose sins you retain are retained" (John 20:21–23). *Receive Penance w/a contrite heart*

Every sin we commit not only affects us personally, but also has social ramifications (even sins that don't seem to be "hurting anyone else"). Sin is a turning away from grace and a disruption of our union with God that weakens our ability to love; thus it hurts us and others. The sacrament of Reconciliation restores us to God's grace and friendship as well as reconciles us with the community of believers, our brothers and sisters whom we are called to love (CCC 1468–1470). *followed by peace & serenity of conscience. A true "spiritual resurrection"*

Sacrament of Reconciliation: Step by Step

1. Examine Our Conscience
According to the *Catechism*, our conscience is a law inscribed by God on the human heart that calls us to love and to choose good and avoid evil (CCC 1776). Before we can ask forgiveness though, it is important that we first examine our conscience to identify how our relationship with God is out of balance. How do we do that? Again from the *Catechism*, the education or forming of one's conscience is a lifelong task guided by reason, the light of the Word of God (or the will of God in Scripture), prayer, the gifts of the Holy Spirit, and the witness and advice of others, and conformed to the moral teachings of the Church (CCC 1783–1785).

2. Confess Our Sins
To obtain forgiveness, we need to have sorrow for our sins and desire to turn away from evil and toward God. When we have examined our consciences and recognized the sin in our lives, we then confess our sins to a priest. Perfect contrition arises from our love for God and the desire to never hurt him instead of from our fear of punishment. Grave sins committed knowingly should be confessed immediately as these destroy charity in the heart by seriously rejecting and violating God's law (CCC 1776). Once these sins are absolved, one can again receive the Eucharist and its much-needed graces.

3. Express Contrition
After we've examined our consciences and confessed our sins, we express our sorrow for them by praying the Act of Contrition and asking for forgiveness and absolution. While it may seem to be a small gesture, in reality interior repentance is intended to be a radical reorientation of our whole life, a return to God with all our heart, a turning away from sin, and the resolution to change one's life with hope in God's mercy and grace.

Act of Contrition: *O my God, I am heartily sorry for having offended you, and I detest all my sins, because of your just punishments, but most of all because they offend you, my God, who are all good and worthy of all my love. I firmly resolve, with the help of your grace, to sin no more and to avoid the near occasions of sin. Amen.*

4. Receive Absolution

The priest, representing Christ and bringing his forgiveness, absolves us from our sins with these words: *"God, the Father of mercies, through the death and Resurrection of his Son has reconciled the world to himself and sent the Holy Spirit among us for the forgiveness of sins; through the ministry of the Church may God give you pardon and peace, and I absolve you from your sins in the name of the Father and of the Son and of the Holy Spirit."*

Additional Resources

FROM THE *CATECHISM*

"The confessor [the priest] is not the master of God's forgiveness but its servant" (CCC 1466). He forgives sin in the name of Jesus Christ.

FROM SCRIPTURE

Psalm 51:10—"Create in me a clean heart, O God. And renew a right spirit within me."

Psalm 130—A song of ascents. "Out of the depths I call to you, LORD; LORD, hear my cry! May your ears be attentive to my cry for mercy. If you, LORD, mark our sins, LORD, who can stand? But with you is forgiveness and so you are revered. I wait with longing for the LORD, my soul waits for his word. My soul looks for the LORD more than sentinels for daybreak. More than sentinels for daybreak, let Israel look for the LORD, for with the LORD is kindness, with him is full redemption, and God will redeem Israel from all their sins."

Luke 15:11–32—Parable of the Prodigal Son

John 8:2–11—The Woman Caught in Adultery: Jesus said, "Let the one among you who is without sin cast the first stone." And in response, they went away one by one. Jesus said to her, "Woman, where are they? Has no one condemned you?" She said, "No one, sir." Then Jesus said, "Neither do I condemn you. Go and from now on sin no more."

FROM CHURCH DOCUMENTS

John Paul II, *Reconciliation and Penance*, 1984.

John Paul II, *Rich in Mercy*, 1980.

Reflection Questions

Outside of a church setting, where have you experienced forgiveness? Has this happened more than once? Does it happen regularly?

What has been your most recent experience of the sacrament of Reconciliation?

How do the Church's teachings guide our consciences? What other sources are there in your life that you rely on for guidance as Catholics?

Do you have any fears that have kept you from approaching this sacrament? What do you think are the origins of these fears? How can these obstacles be removed?

How often should we confess our sins?

My Reflections

Communal celebration, CC 1482

My Reflections cont'd.

VII. Vocation

What am I supposed to do with my life? It is an important question that most of us ask in terms of career choices, living situations, marriage partners, and so on. As Catholics we ask a similar question that goes to an even more fundamental aspect: What am I *called* to do with my life?

The word *vocation* comes from the Latin word meaning "to call." Not that long ago, the term *vocation* was used to indicate a call to religious life: "I think I have a vocation to become a priest." Today, however, we use the term to mean how all of us are being "called to live by God." Regardless of what "state" we are called to—whether we are vowed religious, married, or single—all baptized Christians are called to the shared vocation of being disciples of Jesus Christ. Ultimately, there is a very personal dimension to the issue of our vocation that asks, "How is God calling me to play a particular role in building his Kingdom?" In that way the discernment of our own personal vocation leads us not to the question, "What do I want from God?" but, "What does God want for me?"

Exactly how are we supposed to discern that? By an awareness developed through praying, seeking counsel, and being alert in the circumstances life brings us, we can become more attuned to God's call. Pope John Paul II spoke eloquently on the topic of lay vocation, saying that all states of life, including single and married, share in "the universal call to holiness in the perfection of love. They are different yet complementary....The fundamental objective of the formation of the lay faithful is an ever-clearer discovery of one's vocation, and an ever-greater willingness to live it out....This personal vocation and mission defines the dignity and the responsibility of each member of the lay faithful" (*Christifideles Laici* 58).

Single

While many people's life plans include getting married, it is important to remember that, for Christians, there is nothing "incomplete" about the single state. Regardless of whether we are on a path toward eventual marriage or not, the vocation of single Catholics is to represent Christ through a loving gift of themselves wherever they are and in whatever they do. In many ways those who are single are often more free to listen to God's call and let it lead them wherever necessary.

The baptized, by regeneration and the anointing of the Holy Spirit, are consecrated as a spiritual house and a holy priesthood, that through all their Christian activities they may offer spiritual sacrifices and proclaim the marvels of him who has called them out of darkness into his wonderful life" (*Lumen Gentium* 10).

Married

The majority of men and women are called by God to the vocation of marriage. In a world that often fixates on wedding celebrations, it is important to keep in mind that as Catholics we treat marriage as a sacrament in which a couple publicly binds themselves together in the presence of God and the community for life. It is a vocation to holiness in which the spouses call one another on to greater holiness and openness to the gift of life. "The state of marriage, with the help of God's grace, can be a particularly blessed and grace-filled state," said St. Francis de Sales. "For in it the husband and wife co-operate in God's creation of new human beings and raise souls who may bless and praise Him for all eternity."

Many people are shocked to learn that in entering a covenant of marriage, is not the priest or deacon who acts as the minister. Instead it is the spouses who mutually confer upon each other the sacrament of Matrimony. The priest and the Church assembly act as their witnesses. The Holy Spirit seals their covenant and is the source of their love and strength to live out their vows in mutual fidelity (CCC 1621–1637). Unity, indissolubility, and openness to life are essential to the Catholic sacrament of Marriage. "The Christian home is the place where children receive the first proclamation of the faith. For this reason, the family home is rightly called 'the domestic church,' a community of grace and prayer" (CCC 1664, 1666).

Ordained

By virtue of our Baptism, each one of us is called to share in Christ's priestly, kingly, and prophetic offices (CCC 897–913). But while all believers are through Baptism priests, some are called to serve the Church as Christ himself did. With the sacrament of Holy Orders, Christ entrusted his ministerial mission to the apostles until the end of time. This sacrament continues to be exercised in the Church; thus, it is the sacrament of apostolic ministry. "The ministerial priesthood is at the service of the common priesthood of all believers," helping to unfold the graces within us from Baptism. It is a very important sacrament by which Christ unceasingly builds up and leads his Church, especially since most other sacraments depend upon an ordained minister (CCC 1536, 1547).

God created us uniquely, with special gifts and backgrounds, and asks us to carefully discern how to faithfully live out his call in our lives. Beyond calling us to a particular state of life, God has a particular call for each one of us, a personal vocation in this world. What is your personal vocation?

Additional Resources

FROM THE *CATECHISM*

God himself is the author of marriage." Since God created man and woman, their mutual love is an image of God's love for humanity. As a sacrament of the Church, marriage is not a purely human institution, but comes from the hand of the Creator (CCC 1603–1605).

Only a baptized man validly receives sacred ordination. The Lord Jesus chose men to form the college of the twelve apostles, and the apostles did the same when they chose collaborators to succeed them in their ministry.... The Church recognizes herself to be bound by this choice made by the Lord himself" (CCC 1577).

FROM SCRIPTURE

Isaiah 43:1b—"Fear not, for I have redeemed you; I have called you by name; you are mine."

Ephesians 5:25–26—"Husbands, love your wives, just as Christ loved the Church and gave himself up for her to make her holy...."

1 Corinthians 12:4–5, 27–28—"There are different kinds of gifts, but the same Spirit. There are different kinds of service, but the same Lord....Now you are the body of Christ, and each one of you is a part of it. And in the Church God has appointed first of all apostles, second prophets, third teachers, then workers of miracles, also those having gifts of healings, those able to help others, those with gifts of administration, and those speaking in different kinds of tongues."

Isaiah 6:8—"Then I heard the voice of the Lord saying, 'Whom shall I send? And who will go for us?' And I said, 'Here am I. Send me!'"

FROM CHURCH DOCUMENTS

Vatican II, *Lumen Gentium*, 1964.

John Paul II, *Christifideles Laici* (On the Laity), 1988.

Reflection Questions

All baptized have been given gifts by God to use in the service of others. As an individual (single, married, or religious; parent or not), what are your duties as a Christian?

Do you see marriage as a sacrament? Is it important to get married "in the Church"?

Whether a spouse shares your beliefs might affect your relationship. How? And how might it affect your relationship with your family?

What is the role of those who are ordained or vowed religious in the community?

Acknowledging the increased demand for and decreased numbers of clergy and religious, what more can we do today to support their vocations? How can they support us in ours?

How is God calling you today? Has your time in LANDINGS helped clarify that call?

How will you respond to this call?

My Reflections

My Reflections cont'd.

VIII. Suffering, Death, and Resurrection

For many, the existence of suffering is the ultimate obstacle to faith. How can the God we described in previous weeks who is all loving, compassionate, and forgiving also allow tremendous suffering to occur? This is a topic that philosophers and theologians have wrestled with for millennia. How do we make sense of such a stark contradiction?

As Christians this dilemma is made tangible in the person of Jesus Christ. In Jesus, God became flesh. Through Jesus, God experienced what it meant to be human, including suffering and death. It is through this that we know that we are not alone. God understands our humanity and our pain.

"For you have been called for this purpose, since Christ also suffered for you, leaving you an example for you to follow in his steps...and he himself bore our sins in his body on the cross, so that we might die to sin and live to righteousness; for by his wounds you were healed" (1 Peter 2:21, 24).

Through the crucifixion and Resurrection, the stark contradiction that exists between an all-loving and compassionate God and the suffering in the world is reconciled. Through Jesus, God became one of us, and with the crucifixion he entered into our suffering so we know that we are not alone in our pain. The Resurrection extends our hope beyond this fallen world into a pure love and wholeness in the next. We are a Resurrection people.

In the first week, we read that God made us to one day complete our stories with him eternally. Because of the Resurrection of Jesus, our death is not an end to our life, but the beginning of a new life with God.

In his earthly ministry, Jesus healed the whole person, body, mind, and spirit. He sought to alleviate suffering. We know he healed the blind and the sick. But his healing was not limited to the physical; he also healed spiritually—"go forth and sin no more."

The Church, in the sacrament of the Anointing of the Sick, seeks to strengthen the baptized in their serious illness or old age. It consists of the anointing of the forehead and hands accompanied by prayer for courage and the gift of peace from the Holy Spirit. If death is near, it also forgives sin if the person is unable to obtain forgiveness through the sacrament of Penance, and prepares the person for passing over to eternal life.

Death is not an end, but a transition to a beautiful life with God for those who desire it. When we die, each of us will be judged based on our faith and works (CCC 1021–1022, 1051). By creating us with free will, God gives us the choice of communion with him through the decisions we make during our lives on earth. We are saved by grace alone, but we show our love through our obedience to God in this life.

Heaven, Hell, and Purgatory

Of course, any discussion about sickness, death, and eternal life must include the topics of heaven and hell. What are they? Are they places? If so, where are they? As children we may have believed that heaven is beyond the sky and hell deep beneath our feet. As adults, it might be more helpful to consider heaven as a "mystery of blessed communion with God" that is beyond all understanding. Heaven refers to "the state of supreme and definitive happiness" that is a result of seeing, "face to face," God who is love and for whom we were made (1 Corinthians 13:12; Comp. 209; CCC 1023–1026). Pope Benedict XVI says it is "the place where the innocent no longer suffer, where the strongest no longer win all the arguments, and where gossip, cruelty, and misery come to an end" (*God Is Near Us*, 2001).

Catholics believe that God's mercy and love are great and that "he desires all to be saved and to come to a knowledge of the truth" (1 Timothy 2:4). But God created humans with free will to accept or reject love and goodness. For those who reject him, hell exists and is eternal. Holy Scripture warns that our lives here will reflect our choice—"He who does not love remains in death. Anyone who hates his brother is a murderer, and you know that no murderer has eternal life abiding in him" (1 John 3:14–15). Pope Benedict XVI calls hell "the loneliness into which love can no longer reach" (Ratzinger, *Introduction to Christianity*, 1990). The *Catechism* calls it "the state of definitive self-exclusion from communion with God and the blessed"; those in hell have chosen a life separated from God (CCC 1033–1035). *hell*

The Church also believes in a state of purification, or cleansing, for those who died in "grace and friendship" with God, but still have obstacles in their souls to enjoying the bliss of complete union with the Trinity. This state is called "purgatory" because we are purged of those things within us that are not holy. This is to prepare us to enter God's presence in the joy and light of heaven (CCC 1030–1032). *The final purification or purgatory*

If we desire an eternal life with God and seek after goodness with a sincere heart and childlike spirit, and our life reflects this desire, we can trust in God's love and mercy, and his promise for eternity, that "no eye has seen, no ear has heard, and no mind has imagined what God has prepared for those who love him" (1 Corinthians 2:9).

Additional Resources

FROM THE *CATECHISM*

When someone falls ill, there are different ways of dealing with the pain and suffering. Some experience "anguish, self-absorption, sometimes even despair and revolt against God. It can also make a person more mature, helping him discern in his life what is not essential so that he can turn toward that which is" (CCC 1501). *[handwritten: illness provokes a search for God and a return to him]*

God Almighty in view of suffering: CCC 272–274 *[handwritten: nothing is impossible w/o God]*

Christ's redemptive death in the plan of salvation: CCC 599–618 *[handwritten: was part of the mystery of God's plan]* *[handwritten: God's death]*

Judgment, Heaven, Purgatory, and Hell: CCC 1020–1065

FROM SCRIPTURE

1 Corinthians 13:12—"For now we see in a mirror dimly, but then face to face; now I know in part, but then I will know fully just as I also have been fully known."

1 Thessalonians 5:16–18—"Rejoice always; pray without ceasing; in everything give thanks; for this is God's will for you in Christ Jesus."

John 14:2—Jesus said, "In my Father's house are many dwelling places; if it were not so, I would have told you; for I go to prepare a place for you."

FROM CHURCH DOCUMENTS

John Paul II, *The Christian Meaning of Human Suffering* (*Salvifici Doloris*), 1984.

[handwritten: To believe in the Holy Spirit is to profess that the Holy Spirit is one of the persons of the Holy Trinity consubstancial with the Father and the Son]

Reflection Questions

How have I handled the suffering in my life? Did it bring me closer to God, or did it push me away?

How have I witnessed others handle suffering? How do I react when suffering occurs to someone close to me, as opposed to someone I don't know? What has that taught me?

Do I believe that some suffering can contain some value?

Do I believe that heaven is what I was truly made for, my true home, and that I will be fully happy there with God, or does heaven sound boring?

Have I ever experienced some small sense of heaven or hell here on earth? What was that like?

Have loved ones close to you passed away? How have your losses affected your life and faith?

My Reflections

IX. The Catholic Life

Perhaps here at LANDINGS you've experienced a genuine sense of spiritual connectedness and hope during our meetings, but find it's been difficult to extend that same feeling outside our gatherings and into your daily life.

Our hopes and beliefs can be deeply comforting and inspiring in settings such as these but difficult to hold on to amidst the confusion and messiness of everyday life. It is very common for people to struggle with how to live out their faith. No faith journey is without its struggles, doubts, and wrong turns. As we live our vocation as Christians, we will encounter situations in the world where we need support and guidance on how to act. That is precisely why we take time to gather together in community, so that we can strengthen each other in these struggles.

One of the beautiful gifts of the Catholic faith is that it encompasses two thousand years of tradition and scholarship, not to mention countless holy men and women who have come before us and who now pray for us from heaven. We are never alone or without tremendous resources on this journey.

As our time with LANDINGS comes to an end, how do we step out to be active and authentic followers of Jesus, not only in our parishes on Sundays, but also in our work, neighborhoods, and families? This is the challenge we face, but we don't face this challenge alone. God in his Holy Spirit is with us through our relationships and our community of faith, as well as through the sacramental and spiritual life of the Church, to give us wisdom and to comfort us as we each continue to write the story of our lives.

How Does My Faith Inform My Daily Life?

In the struggle to live out our beliefs in the everyday world, our Catholic faith provides a helpful lens informed by countless lives and thousands of years of thought, experience, and tradition through which we perceive the world. This rich history, tradition, and scholarship are tremendous assets that help us assess the world we live in and make decisions that are consistent with our faith. Our faith equips us to address moral and political questions we inevitably encounter by helping us develop well-formed consciences. "We Catholics have a lifelong obligation to form our consciences in accord with human reason and enlightened by the teaching of Christ as it comes to us through the Church" (USCCB, *The Challenges of Forming Consciences for Faithful Citizenship*, 2007).

Few of us are ever confronted with the extreme moral dilemmas we sometimes see in the news, but that doesn't mean the decisions we make in our daily lives don't have a very real moral dimension. Quite the contrary, so much of the "stuff" of our lives—our relationships, our careers, our families—contain very real moral components; the Catholic faith offers teachings about morality and how we live our lives in the world.

Often when Catholic teaching is talked about in the media or even among our circle of friends and coworkers, it is decontextualized and doesn't seem to make sense. "Why is the Church so uptight about sex?" or "Why is the Church so conservative on the issue of abortion and contraception and so liberal on workers' rights and immigration?" Sound familiar? Perhaps there are questions you've asked yourself.

The fundamental idea that grounds all Catholic moral teaching is that all human life is sacred. Our lives are sacred. We are all created good, in the image and likeness of God. We have the right to be treated with dignity and given what we need to flourish. We also have the responsibility to advocate for the rights of others to live a good life, to be free from poverty, and to have opportunities for work.

"God created man in his image, in the divine image he created him; male and female he created them" (Genesis 1:27).

Jesus said to them, "You shall love the Lord, your God, with all your heart, with all your soul, and with all your mind. This is the greatest and the first commandment. The second is like it; you shall love your neighbor as yourself" (Matthew 22:37–39).

These are powerful and—in some respects—radical teachings. As beloved children of God, we have lives that are sacred and have inherent dignity, regardless of our abilities, our socioeconomic status, or our phase of life. The Church's teachings are holistic because they challenge us to live as if all human life is sacred from the moment of conception to the moment of natural death, cultivating an awareness of God in every aspect of our lives.

All of the social teachings of the Church flow from this notion. We are built for relationship. The fundamental relationship we experience is that of marriage and family, which the Church sees as the basic institution of society. We live out relationships in community, whether the community of our work, our neighbors, our friends, or our family. We are responsible for promoting the common good, with particular attention to the rights of the poor, the dignity of those who work, and the care of all God's creation. We do this because we are in relationship, in solidarity, with the entire human family (USCCB, *Sharing Catholic Social Teaching: Challenges and Directions*, 1998).

As children of God, our bodies are temples of the Holy Spirit, dwelling places for Christ. Consequently, any action or practice that objectifies another person for us and treats him or her as less than a dwelling place for God (lust, pornography, sexual abuse) should be avoided. All Christians—married, single, religious, and ordained—are called to pursue a life of holiness and the virtue of chastity. "Chastity means the successful integration of sexuality within the person and thus the inner unity of ourselves in our bodily and spiritual being" (CCC 2337). Out of love for our partner, we should desire to experience our love in the way God intended, in accordance with our dignity. "God created both the body and sex for good. Hence, we do not ap-

)ach sexuality with fear or with hostility to the flesh. It is a gift of God by ich men and women participate in his saving plan and respond to his call holiness" (*United States Catholic Catechism for Adults*, 2006).

rried love is also created in the image and likeness of God. The Father, n, and Holy Spirit give themselves to each other in a mutual community love. Similarly, married love is a mutual community of self-giving love tween the spouses, where they are no longer two, but one flesh. Because e marriage vows represent a lifelong sacramental bond between a Chris- n man and a Christian woman, the Church teaches that the most intimate cual expression should be reserved for marriage.

In the Public Square

ır Catholic faith also demands us to examine our morality beyond our own rsonal relationships. The Church calls us to be people of action, engaged the world, to promote the sacredness of every human being. As a result, a nsistent ethic of life should guide all Catholic engagement in political life. is consistent ethic of life is what informs the Church's opposition to abor- n, euthanasia, human cloning, and the destruction of human embryos research. This teaching also compels us as Catholics to oppose genocide, ture, unjust war, and the death penalty, as well as to pursue peace and help overcome poverty, racism, and other conditions that demean human .

have the responsibility to participate in the democratic process and to faithful Catholic citizens. As the bishops have written: "A Catholic moral mework does not easily fit the ideologies of right or left, nor the plat- rms of any party. Our values are often not 'politically correct.' Believers called to be a community of conscience within the larger society and to t public life by the values of Scripture and the principles of Catholic social ıching. Our responsibility is to measure all candidates, policies, parties, d platforms by how they protect or undermine the life, dignity, and rights the human person, whether they protect the poor and vulnerable, and vance the common good" (*Faithful Citizenship*, 2003).

are called to participate in building the Kingdom of God, promoting ve, justice, and mercy for the whole world. Our faith teaches us that the ıgdom will be realized partially on earth, and permanently in heaven. At e end of our mortal lives—our love story with God—we believe we will ex- rience the joy of fulfilling our eternal destiny, to be in blessed communion th Love itself.

Seven Themes of Catholic Social Teaching
(From the United States Conference of Catholic Bishops)

Life and Dignity of the Human Person

The Catholic Church proclaims that human life is sacred and that the dignity of the human person is the foundation of a moral vision for society. This belief is the foundation of all the principles of our social teaching. In our society, human life is under direct attack from abortion and euthanasia. The value of human life is being threatened by cloning, embryonic stem-cell research, and the death penalty. The intentional targeting of civilians in war or terrorist attacks is always wrong. Catholic teaching also calls on us to work to avoid war. Nations must protect the right to life by finding increasingly effective ways to prevent conflicts and to resolve them by peaceful means. We believe that every person is precious, that people are more important than things, and that the measure of every institution is whether it threatens or enhances the life and dignity of the human person.

Call to Family, Community, and Participation

The person is not only sacred but also social. How we organize our society—in economics and politics, in law and policy—directly affects human dignity and the capacity of individuals to grow in community. Marriage and the family are the central social institutions that must be supported and strengthened, not undermined. We believe people have a right and a duty to participate in society, seeking together the common good and well-being of all, especially the poor and vulnerable.

Rights and Responsibilities

Our Catholic tradition teaches that human dignity can be protected and a healthy community can be achieved only if human rights are protected and responsibilities are met. Therefore, every person has a fundamental right to life and a right to those things required for human decency. Corresponding to these rights are duties and responsibilities—to one another, to our families, and to the larger society.

Option for the Poor and Vulnerable

A basic moral test is how our most vulnerable members are faring. In a society marred by deepening divisions between rich and poor, our tradition recalls the story of the Last Judgment (Matthew 25:31–46) and instructs us put the needs of the poor and vulnerable first.

The Dignity of Work and the Rights of Workers

The economy must serve people, not the other way around. Work is more than a way to make a living; it is a form of continuing participation in God's creation. If the dignity of work is to be protected, then the basic rights of workers must be respected—the right to productive work, to decent and fair wages, to the organization and joining of unions, to private property, and economic initiative.

Solidarity

We are one human family, whatever our national, racial, ethnic, economic, and ideological differences. We are our brothers' and sisters' keepers, wherever they may be. Loving our neighbor has global dimensions in a shrinking world. At the core of the virtue of solidarity is the pursuit of justice and peace. Pope Paul VI taught that "if you want peace, work for justice." The Gospel calls us to be peacemakers. Our love for all our sisters and brothers demands that we promote peace in a world surrounded by violence and conflict.

Care for God's Creation

We show our respect for the Creator by our stewardship of creation. Care for the earth is not just an Earth Day slogan; it is a requirement of our faith. We are called to protect people and the planet, living our faith in relationship with all of God's creation. This environmental challenge has fundamental moral and ethical dimensions that cannot be ignored.

—*Forming Consciences for Faithful Citizenship* 40–56

Additional Resources

FROM SCRIPTURE

Matthew 5:2–12—The Beatitudes

Luke 16:19–31—The Rich Man and Lazarus

Luke 10:29–37—The Good Samaritan

FROM CHURCH DOCUMENTS

John XXIII, *Peace on Earth (Pacem in Terris)*, 1963.

John Paul II, *Gospel of Life (Evangelium Vitae)*, 1995.

John Paul II, *The Christian Family in the Modern World (Familiaris Consortio)*, 1981.

Leo XIII, *On the Condition of Labor (Rerum Novarum)*, 1891.

Paul VI, *Of Human Life (Humanae Vitae)*, 1968.

Vatican II, *On the Church in the Modern World (Gaudium et Spes)*, 1965.

USCCB, *Sharing Catholic Social Teaching: Challenges and Directions*, 1998.

USCCB, *Always Our Children: A Pastoral Message to Parents of Homosexual Children*, 1997.

USCCB, *Forming Consciences for Faithful Citizenship*, 2007.

USCCB, *Marriage: Love and Life in the Divine Plan*, 2009.

Reflection Questions

Did what you read about the Church's moral teachings surprise you? Why or why not? Did it contradict anything you thought you already knew?

Has your time in LANDINGS altered how you understand your responsibilities as a Christian? Or as a parent, spouse, or family member?

Have you ever thought about how your own conscience has been formed? What values, beliefs, and personal experiences informed it? How are they consistent with or differ from the values we've spoke of here?

How should a faithful Catholic develop his or her conscience? What role do the Church's teachings on equality, justice, and the vulnerable play in your decision making? Are there other factors that come into consideration?

Do you agree that the Church promotes a consistent view on the value of human life? What teachings are difficult for you to accept?

My Reflections

My Reflections cont'd.

X. Christian Prayer

As we've discussed throughout LANDINGS, our faith life is centered around our relationship with God. As in any good relationship there must be consistent communication for that relationship to grow and flourish. In a very real sense that is exactly what prayer is. St. Teresa of Avila called prayer "a conversation with One who loves us." In this section, we examine Christian prayer. Times of personal prayer, Scripture reading, and experiences of God's presence in our daily lives and in the sacraments are essential parts of our religious lives.

Our loving Father constantly seeks us so that we might grow closer to him. Prayer too is a gift from God that he inspires in us, inviting us to encounter him. The *Catechism* defines prayer as "the raising of one's mind and heart to God, or the petition of good things from him in accord with his will" and a "personal and living relationship" with him (Comp. 534; CCC 2558–2565, 2590).

Jesus teaches us that to truly pray, we must strive to have these dispositions: "purity of heart that seeks the Kingdom and forgives one's enemies, bold and filial faith that goes beyond what we feel and understand, and watchfulness that protects the disciple from temptation" (Comp. 544; CCC 2608–2614, 2621).

How to Pray?

Always helping us toward our eternal destinies, God is so good that he even teaches us how to pray: "We do not know how to pray as we ought" (Romans 8:26), but the Holy Spirit teaches us from within so we should call on him always.

The Church describes the Our Father as "the summary of the whole Gospel" and the prayer "for which there is no substitute" (Comp. 578). Many of us simply pray this prayer every Sunday at Mass without giving much thought to what we are saying and asking God for. To better understand and reinvigorate your praying of this prayer, read the *Cathechism* 2759–2865.

An often-misunderstood aspect of the Catholic spiritual tradition is our devotion to Mary. As the mother of Jesus, she has uniquely cooperated with the Holy Spirit and is uniquely close to her Son. She is the channel of all God's gifts, so the Church prays to her and with her so that Mary may pray for us to be holy like her and to lead us to Jesus. Similarly misunderstood is the Catholic tradition of saints. We do not worship the saints or pray to them as gods. For Catholics, the saints are also models of prayer for us. They are holy men and women down through the ages who have had special relationships with the Lord. We ask them to pray for us and to intercede for us so that we may give glory to God with our lives and someday enjoy eternity in God's presence as they do now (Comp. 561–564; CCC 2673–2693).

POPULAR DEVOTIONS

The Holy Rosary: For almost a thousand years, the Rosary has been regarded as one of the most powerful prayers that the Church has been blessed with. The Rosary is a means of meditating upon the Gospel. The mysteries make up a "compendium of the Gospel" as they recount very important events of Jesus' life. We pray the Apostles' Creed, the Our Father, and the Glory Be in the Rosary, but the heart of the Rosary is the Hail Mary.

The first half of the Hail Mary is taken directly from Scripture: "Hail Mary, full of grace, the Lord is with thee; blessed art thou among women, and blessed is the fruit of thy womb, Jesus" (Luke 1:28, 42). The second half—"Holy Mary, Mother of God, pray for us sinners, now and at the hour of our death. Amen"—simply acknowledges that Mary is the mother of Jesus and asks her to intercede for us since she has been uniquely blessed by God.

The Stations of the Cross: When praying the Stations of the Cross, the faithful "make in spirit...a pilgrimage to the chief scenes of Christ's suffering and death" (*The Catholic Encyclopedia;* available at www.newadvent.org). One usually moves from one image of a Passion scene to another, meditating on Christ's love and its impact on our lives.

Novena: This is a nine-day prayer (to the Holy Spirit, Jesus, Mary, or a saint) performed either privately or with others in order to obtain special graces. *The Catholic Encyclopedia* explains: "The best model and example [of this prayer] was given by Christ himself to the Church in the first Pentecost novena. He himself expressly exhorted the Apostles to make this preparation. And when the young Church had faithfully persevered for nine full days in it, the Holy Ghost came as the precious fruit of this first Christian novena for the feast of the establishment and foundation of the Church" (*Encyclopedia* available at www.newadvent.org).

Additional Resources

FROM THE *CATECHISM*

We all know that our trust in God can be tested when we feel as though our prayers are not being heard. We are challenged to ask ourselves whether we believe that God is our loving Father whom we wish to please out of love and gratitude by doing his will, or whether he is just a means of getting what we want. "If our prayer is united to that of Jesus, we know that he gives us much more than this or that gift. We receive the Holy Spirit who transforms our heart" (Comp. 572, 575; CCC 2725, 2734–2741, 2756).

Christian Prayer—The final section of the *Catechism*, which is about 75 pages long, deals exclusively with prayer. It begins at number 2558.

Prayer in the Christian Life—CCC 2558–2758

The Lord's Prayer—CCC 2759–2865

FROM SCRIPTURE

Matthew 6:9–13—The Our Father

Matthew 7:7–11—"Ask, and it will be given to you; seek, and you will find; knock, and it will be opened to you. For everyone who asks receives, and he who seeks finds, and to him who knocks it will be opened. Or what man is there among you who, when his son asks for a loaf, will give him a stone? Or if he asks for a fish, he will not give him a snake, will he? If you then, being evil, know how to give good gifts to your children, how much more will your Father who is in heaven give what is good to those who ask him!"

Mark 11:25—"Whenever you stand praying, forgive, if you have anything against anyone, so that your Father who is in heaven will also forgive you your transgressions."

Luke 18:1-8—"Then Jesus told them a parable to show that at all times they ought to pray and not to lose heart...."

Romans 8:26—"In the same way the Spirit also helps our weakness; for we do not know how to pray as we should, but the Spirit himself intercedes for us with groanings too deep for words."

1 Thessalonians 5:17—"Pray without ceasing."

James 5:13—"Is anyone among you suffering? Then he must pray. Is anyone cheerful? He is to sing praises."

FROM CHURCH DOCUMENTS

John Paul II, *Apostolic Letter on the Most Holy Rosary (Rosarium Virginis Mariae)*, 2002.

Congregation for the Doctrine of the Faith, "Some Aspects of Christian Meditation," 1989.

Reflection Questions

What method of prayer comes most naturally to you?

Where and how did you learn to pray?

Have you ever felt God's presence when you've prayed?

What does prayer mean to you?

"The Christian family is the first place of education in prayer" (Comp. 565). Do you remember praying with your family? Do you still maintain this practice? What would you like to pass on or do differently in your own family?

What could help you pray the celebration of Mass and the Eucharist better?

My Reflections

My Reflections cont'd.

Every LANDINGS meeting ends with this prayer. It comes from a sermo
by John Henry Newman, a convert to Catholicism who eventuall
became a cardinal and who is now on the road to being declared
saint.

Closing Prayer

May [Christ] support us all the day long,
Til the shades lengthen, and the evening comes,
And the busy world is hushed, and the fever of life is over,
And our work is done!
Then, in His mercy, may He give us
Safe lodging, and a holy rest, and peace at the last!

—Blessed John Henry Cardinal Newman

May 13th - Fr. Phil
June 10 - Pot Luck - Robin's Lu